Granny's Cranberry Sauce

by Bronwyn Evans

Illustrated by Maribel Suarez

Editorial Offices: Glenview, Illinois • Parsippany, New Jersey • New York, New York
Sales Offices: Needham, Massachusetts • Duluth, Georgia • Glenview, Illinois
Coppell, Texas • Sacramento, California • Mesa, Arizona

It is Thanksgiving Day.
The turkey is hot and brown.
The pies are sweet and spicy.
Mother and Granny go into the kitchen.
They will make something special!

"What are you doing?" asks Jasmine.
"We are making cranberry sauce,"
says Granny.
"May I watch?" asks Jasmine.
"Yes," says Granny, "I will teach you
how to make my special sauce."

Mother says, "When I was little, Granny let me help her cook. That is how I learned to cook."
Jasmine says, "Now I will learn how to cook!"

cranberries

Jasmine touches a little red berry.
"This is a cranberry," Granny tells her.
"May I taste it?" asks Jasmine.
"Not yet," answers Granny.
"Cranberries are very sour!"

sugar

water

"Let's make them sweet," says Mother.
Granny pours the berries into a pan.
"Now add sugar," Mother says.
Jasmine puts sugar on the cranberries.
"Now add water," says Granny.

stove

Granny puts the pan on the stove.
"Listen to the cranberries," says Granny.
The hot berries pop and bubble.
Jasmine laughs!
"The cranberries are singing!" she says.

cranberry sauce

The cranberry sauce is made.
"This Thanksgiving is special," says Granny.
"Jasmine learned to make cranberry sauce!"
"You are special, Granny," says Jasmine.